THE MASS

The Story of God's
Everlasting Love for You!

Hope and Purpose Ministries
Fr. William Maestri

The Mass: The Story of God's Everlasting Love for YOU!
Written by Fr. William Maestri
Copyright © 2017 by Hope and Purpose Ministries
Printed in the United States

ISBN: 1979530467
ISBN-13: 978-1979530460

CONTENTS

LETTER FROM THE FOUNDER AND PRESIDENT
OF HOPE AND PURPOSE MINISTRIES

Dear Reader,

Through Hope and Purpose Ministries, we are working to further the ministry of Jesus to proclaim the Kingdom of God (Matthew 10:7), encourage others that God has a plan and purpose for their lives (Jeremiah 29:11), and to help heal the broken-hearted (John 10:10b). Our mission is to participate in the New Evangelization through preaching, teaching, leading retreats and parish missions, and helping people foster the baptism of the Holy Spirit. Our mission came from three Scriptures:

"As you go, make this proclamation: 'The kingdom of heaven is at hand.'" —Matthew 10:7, NAB

"I came so that they might have life and have it more abundantly." —John 10:10b, NAB

"For I know well the plans I have in mind for you…plans for your welfare and not for   woe, so as to give you a future of hope." —Jeremiah 29:11, NAB

In support of our mission statement and core Scriptures, Hope and Purpose Ministries has five main initiatives that we work toward through our ministry efforts: Prayer, New Evangelization, Urban Evangelization, International Outreach, and Ecumenical Harmony.

You can learn more about Hope and Purpose Ministries and each of our initiatives at our website: www.HopeAndPurpose.org.

I have spoken across the globe; from Europe to Africa to Brazil to Canada and throughout the United States, and I have learned that people everywhere are hungry for God. They yearn to grow closer to God—Father, Son, and Holy Spirit—and to learn to be a better disciple of Christ. Throughout my travels, I have witnessed the strength of people and their determination to carry on in the face of great distress—hunger, political upheaval, and injustice. It is God's mercy and kindness that are revealed in these situations. God is always there for His people. Everyone can call out to God and He will answer them.

With this book on the Mass and prayer, we pray that your spiritual journey will be renewed and refreshed and that you would experience a fuller relationship with Jesus. You can visit our website to learn about our upcoming events and to see our other resources for you. Be sure to read our blog and follow us on social media to become a part of the growing conversation about what God is doing in our world today.

May this book lead to a season of spiritual growth for you and your family and may God continue to bless you abundantly!

Deacon Larry Oney

Founder and President
Hope and Purpose Ministries

The Mass

We human beings love a story; any kind of story: adventure, mystery, stories of great deeds and events, action stories, and yes, love stories. The Bible is a book, or better a library, of the stories between God and human beings. The Bible tells us of all kinds of stories: sin and redemption; bravery and cowardice; obedience and rebellion; self-sacrifice and selfishness; hope and despair; faith and doubt; and the list goes on. The Bible tells stories about real people and the challenges which life presents. We can see ourselves in their struggles, triumphs, failures, and victories. The Bible is <u>not</u> a library of fables and fairy-tales, but a collection of stories about God seeking us and our many responses to the God who wants to be known.

Stories are a vital part of human history. From earliest times when people gathered in caves, to the lonely writer shut away creating the next greatest American novel, there is a powerful force within us that *must* tell and hear stories. Stories connect us to past generations and the complex saga of human experience. We need to feel that we are part of something larger than the individual self. Stories remind us that life is connected to life and draws us outward against the forces of isolation and loneliness.

The talk of stories may strike one as childish, immature, and silly. In time we will grow up and stop telling stories. How sad! When we stop telling stories we lose a crucial part of our humanity, our imagination, our willingness to believe. Even in our computer age, children know the importance of stories. A child tucked in bed for the night makes a profound request "Tell me a story." In the face of darkness and the fear of what lies in the darkness, the child asks to be told a story. The child is asking for someone to say there is a light which shines, an order and meaning to even the night, and there is a security and peace which will not be taken away. The child enters sleep. The power of story, a grace, brings rest. Throughout our lives we need this grace of story to make sense of a world that in too much with us. We need to know that everything will be alright. And work unto good.

In all honesty we must admit that many today, especially the young, find the Mass boring. Why? Too often the Mass is presented as a <u>duty</u> which one must endure in order to avoid serious sin. Fear and guilt are poor substitutions for joy and gratitude. Glum assemblies are a far cry from the Holy Spirit filled communities who shout joyfully to the Lord. The call to 'celebrate'

God's everlasting love seems painfully absent in our churches. The call to sing the Lord's praises is *not* to reduce the Mass to secular entertainment. Rather, when we gather for Mass, we <u>cannot help</u> but lift a shout-filled joy to the God who has done great things for us.

We will now turn our attention to the *story* of the Mass. This may seem to be irreverent, for we do not want to reduce the Mass to a story. Such a reaction may be understandable, such it is to miss the crucial link between the Mass and story. The Mass in the story of God's everlasting love for each human person. This 'love story' was revealed from the beginning of creation and *continues* throughout history into eternity. The maximum revelation of the Divine Love came in the Person of Jesus the Christ. And this revelation **continues** in the Holy Sacrifice of the Mass. God's people are *not* abandoned, rather, the Person of Jesus reveals a Love which is faithful and always *with* and *for* us.

While we now begin our meditation on the *individual* parts on themes of the Mass, we must always remember that the **whole** story of the Mass is greater, supremely greater, that any of its individual parts. The various aspects of the Mass join to form the tremendous story of God's everlasting love for each of us.

William F. Maestri

Entrance Chant

The congregation stands and should face the altar. The priest, deacon, and various lay ministers process to the altar on which the Eucharist will be offered. The *focus* is on the altar on which the bread and wine will become, through the Holy Spirit, the Body and Blood of Jesus Christ.

Greeting

The community of faith begins the sacrifice of the Mass with that most holy of signs; the sign of the Cross. This points to the God who is One and yet a oneness of Three Persons: Father/Creator, Son/Redeemer, and the Holy Spirit/Sanctifier. The sign of the Cross points to God's everlasting love for each person. For it is on the Cross that the saving love of God is revealed. Jesus is the perfect sacrifice on Calvary and the perfect sacrifice on the altar before us.

Penitential Act

To enter deeply into the mystery of God's love, we must call to mind the ways in which we have sinned. We can acknowledge our sins because God is rich in mercy and forgiveness. We need not fear or hide from God. We can come before God with both sorrow and joy. We can dare appear before the judgement of Jesus because it is a judgement of infinite mercy, forgiveness, and healing LOVE. In the presence of Jesus, we can reveal ourselves as we are. We can dare to do this because in the presence of perfect love, all fear is driven out. Our sins effect the Church—the Body of Christ. We seek forgiveness from those whose faith we have weakened; whose hope we have diminished; and form those we failed to love.

Gloria

The great prayer of praise joins our voices with the Heavenly Host at the birth of Jesus, "Glory to God in the highest…". The victory desired by sin and death will not take place. The birth of the Messiah swallows up the sting of death; sin is defeated by amazing grace; the Light shines in the darkness and is not overcome; hope, not despair, carries us forward; and LOVE drives out all fear. The penitential act, by which we seek God's infinite mercy, leads us to the praise of God's glory—forgiving, redeeming love.

Collect

The Church who gathers for worship is a Church who prays. The Collect is the faith community who prays with a spirit of preparation and anticipation for the Word of the Lord and the Gospel of Jesus Christ. The Collect is a prayer which focuses our attention as to the proper response to the coming Word of God.

Liturgy of the Word

In joyful and eager expectation, we sit to <u>listen</u> to the Word of the Lord. We do not simply hear the Word; which is a physiological occurrence, rather, we listen to the Word which is *spiritual*; we are to open our hearts as the Lord speaks to us. The Word of the Lord is *not* read as one would read a newspaper, instead the Word of God is **proclaimed** in the assembly; **to** the assembly requiring a response. And that response is most fitting: "Thanks be to God." One can only be grateful for having been spoken to by God.

The Word is known from the Old Testament, the Psalms, and one of the books in the New Testament after the Four Gospels.

The first reading selected from the Old Testament needs a brief word of exploration. The use of the word 'old' denotes to the modern mind as something which is outdated, obsolete, and of no value. Such is **not** the case when it comes to the Bible. For the use of the term 'old' denotes reverence, honor, and fidelity to truth. The Old Testament is the story of God's fidelity to His promises (Covenant) made to Abraham, Isaac, and Jacob. No matter how unfaithful the Israelites, God remains forever faithful to His Word. Again and again, God seeks His people to once again be faithful and in love with the God who formed them as a people, liberated them from bondage, and the people through whom the Savior will come. God's fidelity to His promises is realized in the Person of Jesus, God's letter (Word) of love to the world.

After the first reading the congregation is invited to express its response to God's Word:

The Responsorial Psalm

The first reading calls for a decision or answer by the faith community. God's Word is not just God speaking to us, God expects us to answer. The Responsorial Psalm is a most fitting way for us to acknowledge the Word and enter into communication with God. The Psalms, many attributed to King David, powerfully express God's people seeking help, forgiveness, and praising the absolute greatness of the Lord.

The Responsorial Psalm is not only the community's response to God's Word in the first reading, the Responsorial Psalm leads the congregation to the second reading selected from the New Testament collection of Holy Spirit-inspired writings.

When Jesus returns to the Father after the Resurrection, He does not abandon the disciples. Jesus' Ascension to the Father brings fourth the sending of the Holy Spirit and the beginning of the Church (Pentecost). The letters and writings of the New Testament provide us with a kind of 'distant mirror' in which we see ourselves. The Church in every time and place faces similar challenges, trials, persecutions, and *the indwelling presence of the Holy Spirit*. Jesus did not leave His Church alone. God's love is a faithful love. And the Divine Love is with the Church into eternity.

For the individual who leaves the Church after Mass, these readings serve as a constant source inspiration, encouragement, and exhortation. We depart the offering of Mass and go into our everyday world. The Holy Spirit power of the Word sustains us in faithful discipleship. Our listening to the Word empowers us to help transform the world into a creation which gives glory to God. We are even thoughtful for the gift of the Word.

Gospel Acclamation

We have been sitting for the first and second readings as well as the Responsorial Psalm, now we **stand** in utmost anticipation of the Gospel; the greatest news ever proclaimed. We lift our voices in union with our bodies as we give a joyful shout "Alleluia, alleluia". We cannot help but declare our praise and thanksgiving for what is about to take place, namely, the Word of salvation has entered the human heart and history. God's saving love has taken on a human face—Jesus.

Gospel Reading

The priest or deacon ascends the pulpit and dares, in fear and trembling, to proclaim, "A reading from the Holy Gospel...". As he is about to declare the Gospel, the priest or deacon makes the sign of the Cross on his forehead, lips, and heart. The sign of the Cross is a prayer for the Holy Spirit purification of one's mind, speech, and will (heart). This sign of the Cross is a recognition of one's unworthiness and the need for courage to speak Gospel truth.

In the assembly gathered the Gospel, the good news, is proclaimed. The Gospel is not good information; not interesting; not a curious speech only for a few. The Good News is just that, namely, news which we must share in word and deed. We cannot keep this news—the victory of Jesus over sin, death, and the powers of darkness—to ourselves. We must proclaim the Gospel to the ends of the earth. The Church as a whole, and each individual Christian, is empowered through the Holy Spirit to make disciples of all nations (evangelize). Our mission field for witnessing to the Gospel is that part and place of the world we can win for Church—home, school, workspace, clubs, and associations. We may not speak with the 'eloquence of angels' but the daily love we show to others proclaims the Good News. Each of us is a vital part of God's ongoing story of love.)

Homily

The Word of God and the Gospel are entrusted to humans; fragile, limited vessels of clay. The one called to preach engages in a form of speech like no other. The homily or sermon comes through the Bible, through the preacher, and addresses the congregation. The sermon or homily is a gift of grace from on high and speaks to each person directly. The words spoken by the preacher may comfort, challenge, and alarm us. The words spoken from the pulpit represent Jesus knocking at the door of our heart. At the preaching of the living Word, the Holy Spirit descends and calls to conversion each heart and the outside world. The preaching of the Word makes present the God who is with and *for us*.

Profession of Faith

After the homily the assembly rises. As individuals and as a community, the **public** expression of faith in the One God who is Father, Son, and Holy Spirit takes place. Our standing together, professing faith in the Trinity, serves as a powerful encouragement to preserve the unity of belief with makes Christ Church. The 'standing together' is a reminder that the Christian journey to God involves a community of faith, the Church. We need each other to support and enrich our shared way of life. We are stronger together than we are alone. The pilgrimage of faith calls us to be companions, to be **Church**.

The 'standing together' in faith challenges us to give public witness to the Father, Son, and Holy Spirit. We do not keep our faith hidden or a secret. We are to loudly profess the love of the Father, the Lordship of Jesus, and the indwelling presence of the Holy Spirit. Such a faith witness is not done with arrogance, moralistic pride, and condemnation. Rather, we live and offer the faith as a gift to enrich public life and the life of each individual.

Prayer of the Faithful

The congregation which stands together in declaring a common faith, *remains standing* as a faith-filled people of prayer. The prayers offered are not just for the Church or there within the walls, but the canopy of prayer by the faithful is **universal**. Prayers are voiced for the universal needs of the Church *and* the urgent needs of the world. Prayer is not bound by geography or limited to specific groups, rather, the God to whom we pray embraces the earth and all within. The God to whom we pray is a God of attentive love. Nothing that happens to us, the Church, and the world is beyond the reach of God's powerful love. From the smallest concern that burdens our heart, to the large events that shake our world, God cares and is mindful of what is good and proper. After each petition we pray, "Lord, hear our prayer." Not only does God listen, God empowers us to work for His blessed purpose.

Liturgy of the Eucharist

We proceed from the Liturgy of the Word to the Liturgy of the Eucharist. We are **not** ending one litany (Word) to start another (Eucharist) with no connection between the two. On the contrary. The Liturgy of the Word and the Eucharist are *united* within the story of God's everlasting love. And the Divine Love is expressed through nourishment. The pulpit and the altar, Scripture and Eucharist come together to feed the hungry soul. Hence, the

Liturgy of the Word and the Liturgy of the Eucharist are <u>not</u> separated but continue into the greatest story ever told—God's everlasting love for us.

Presentation and Preparation of the Gifts

Presentation

The simple gifts of bread, water, and wine are brought forth for the sacrifice of the Mass. These offerings are simple in that they are *basic* to human survival. These fundamental gifts reflect the loving care of God for the precious gift of life. These natural gifts will be offered in gratitude to the Father who is the Giver of all gifts. There simple gifts, through the presence of the Holy Spirit of the consecration, will be transformed into the Body and Blood of Christ. God receives His gifts from the natural order (bread, water, and wine) and elevates them into the supernatural order of grace for our salvation.

Preparation

The gifts presented are received and placed on the altar and prepared for the sacrifice of the Mass. The water is blessed, and small amount is poured into the chalice. This calls to mind the sacrifice of Jesus on the Cross when blood and water came from his side. The chalice and paten upon which the host rest are presented to God with a request for acceptance and blessing. The priest then has his fingers washed as a sign of humility and the need for cleaning. The washing of fingers is the priest's acknowledging his own need to be forgiven by God, and the need to be spiritually purified in order to properly offer the bread and wine which will become the Body and Blood of Christ.

Preface

The Preface is a prayer of preparation and expectation. We are called back to inwardly prepare to participate in the story of God's love which is unfolding before us <u>and</u> within us. The experience of feeling God's tremendous love creates in us a hunger for greater communion with the God who wants to be with us and is for us.

There are a number of Prefaces prayed at the offering of Mass depending on the Eucharistic Prayer on the special occasion for which the Mass is offered. However, there is found in each Preface, namely, the giving of thanks and praise to the Father. The gifts of bread, wine and water which are offered and placed on the altar in recognition that the Father is the Given of all good gifts.

Preface Acclamation

At the end of the Preface and acknowledges the God who gives us gifts, we proclaim God is HOLY. In fact, God is HOLINESS ITSELF. The holy presence of God fills the **whole** of creation. Every aspect of life is holy. Why? Because the God who is holiness itself is the loving Creator who brings everything into existence.

Eucharistic Prayer

During the weekdays and on Sunday there are four regularly prayed Eucharistic Prayers: I (Roman Canon), II, III and IV. There are acceptable Eucharistic Prayers which may be prayed for various occasions and the Mass with children. As we pray the Eucharistic Prayer we do while *kneeling* as a sign of our humility and gratitude for being called into the very presence of our Holy God. Yet, each of our Eucharistic Prayers follows a similar storyline or structure:

- The acknowledgement of God, Father, Son, and Holy Spirit as holy and asking for God's blessing on the gifts offered.
- The calling down of the Holy Spirit upon the gifts to transform them into the Body and Blood of Christ. Through the Holy Spirit the gifts are consecrated, made holy, so as to be acceptable to the Lord.
- The words of Jesus at the Last Supper are repeated by the priest. The bread becomes the Body of Christ and is elevated upward to the glory of God. Likewise, the wine in the chalice becomes the Blood of Christ and lifted upward in the praise of Jesus' saving sacrifice of love on the Cross.

- The world and actions of the priest in union with the congregation are done in loving obedience to Jesus. 'Do this in memory of me.'

Memorial Acclamation

Present in our midst on the altar is the **REAL PRESENCE** of the Body and Blood of Christ. Such a mystery calls us to speak our faith individually and as a community. We profess our faith in the mystery of Jesus' death, resurrection, and return in glory. The Eucharist is our Sacrament of encounter with the crucified, resurrected, and the King of glory who will come again.

As we continue the Eucharistic Prayer the word "memorial" carries us forward. We offer the Eucharist in *memory* of Jesus. There are a number of civic or secular memorial days we celebrate—Independence Day, Thanksgiving, Memorial Day, to name but a few. However, the Mass is a memorial of a totally different kind. Our celebration of national holidays or events is the calling to mind of events or people in the past. Those events or persons *remain* in the past, these civic celebrations can never make really present that which we honor. However powerful, beautiful, and meaningful, the person or event is locked in its historical time and place. Such is *not* the case with the offering of the Mass.

Through the power of the Holy Spirit at the words of consecration, the bread and wine become the **REAL PRESENCE** of the crucified and risen Lord. The congregation becomes *present* with Jesus at the Last Supper and at the foot of the Cross on Calvary. We are in our churches and at the same time we are present at the table of the Lord's Supper. We look upon the altar and are present at the foot of the Cross on that Good Friday. What we remember is *not* frozen in some past time and place, but becomes *present* in our midst.

We continue the Eucharistic Prayer with a series of prayers for various parts of the Body of Christ, the Church:

- For all who are worshipping that they may do as in a proper manner (thankfulness, humility, and reverence)
- For all members of the Church that unity in Christ may be present
- The unity of the Church must be one of charity in solidarity with the Pope as the visible presence of Christ on earth
- We pray for our brothers and sisters in the Lord who have died that they will be welcomed into the presence of our merciful Savior
- We pray for ourselves as part of the Body of Christ that we may be one with the Blessed Mother, Saint Joseph, apostles, and all the Saints in the hope of eternal life.

Concluding Doxology

The Eucharistic Prayer comes to a magnificent end with an acknowledgement and praise of the *glory* (*doxa*) of the Father and the Holy Spirit for the supreme love of Jesus in the sacrifice of the Cross. This love story of God for us underlineu{continues} in the Mass.

Communion Rite

The Eucharistic Prayer, the great prayer of the Church, is not just words but leads us to *action*, namely, the *reception* of the Body and Blood of Christ. We do so by praying together the prayer taught by Jesus.

The Lord's Prayer (see Section 2 for more on this prayer)

Jesus' disciples asked Him to teach them to pray. Jesus' Church is a praying Church and as we prepare to receive His Real Presence, we **stand** in obedience to say:

Our Father: Each human person is made in the image and likeness of God. We are brother and sister to one another with God as *our* Father. We are part of the one family of the Father.

Who art in Heaven: Our Father is above us as to lovingly watch and care for the whole of His creation. This 'being above' is not one of control as it is one of persuading for the good.

Hallowed be thy name: The name, the very essence of God, is holiness itself. As God's people we are to be holy as God is holy. The very name of God calls for us to honor the Divine name with utmost reverence.

Thy Kingdom come: The Kingdom for which we pray is the complete rule of God throughout creation, history, and the human heart. God's rule is one of perfect freedom, justice, and peace.

Thy will be done on earth as it is in Heaven: The Holy Will of the Father is the desire all things, in Heaven and on earth, work toward their proper purpose or fulfillment. The will of the Father is a desire of love and not force. God honors His gift of freedom to us. It is in obedience to God's will that we are free in the best way possible.

Give us this day our daily bread: The Father of all good gifts the One to whom we turn for what we need today. Yesterday is gone and tomorrow is not yet. The gift of today with all its blessings and burdens requires bread- the nourishment and care of our Heavenly Father. We do not face the day alone. The Father who knows us completely will supply for us all our needs.

Forgive us our trespasses: Because God is love we can acknowledge our wrong doing without fear. The hurt we have caused others and the offences against God's holy will we ask forgiveness. We can cleanse our trespasses in truth because of God's mercy.

And we forgive those who trespass against us: God's love and forgiveness calls us to share this forgiving love with those who have offended us. Hatred and violence must not continue. God's forgiving love breaks the deadly cycle of destruction. The world operates by the love of power, the Christian lives by the power of love.

Lead us not into temptation: we pray for the Fathers grace to withstand the turmoil of the 'end days'. Many will turn away from Jesus and His Church. We petition for the courage to stand firm with Jesus the Christ.

Deliver us from evil: As the return of Jesus at the end of the world draws near, the powers of darkness (Satan) becomes more determined to lead many of the faithful along the path of infidelity.

After the *Our Father* we petition the Lord for deliverance from every evil, the gift of peace, the Divine Mercy, liberated from the bondage of sin and the anxiety which sin brings, as we with the blessed hope of the Lord's Second Coming. We make these petitions because of the trust we have in the King of glory whose power is everlasting.

Sign of Peace

The first gift of the Risen Christ to His disciples after the resurrection was peace. The peace of Christ is not the false peace offered by the world. The world's peace comes by denying Jesus as Lord and following the gospel of earthly power. Such a gospel does not provide light and life and peace. Only the Gospel of Jesus offers a peace which no can take away.

The peace of Christ we receive is also a peace to be shared. We cannot bring our gifts to the altar and receive the Lord with a heart filled with anger, resentment, and vengeance. Within the congregation, from family members to strangers, we express the peace of Christ, so we may receive the Lord worthily.

Lamb of God

Jesus is the perfect sacrifice who takes away all sin for all time, Jesus is the One who is offered up to the Father *and* the One who makes the offering of Himself. Jesus is the Eternal High Priest as well as the 'once for all' sacrifice which for mercy and peace.

Invitation to Communion

The priest elevates the host and the chalice and declares that the bread and wine, now the Body and Blood of Christ, is the sinless Lamb who takes away the sins of the world through the Cross. We who are called and come forth are blessed to be nourished by this Second Meal.

In deepest humility we acknowledge our unworthiness and Jesus' infinite mercy which heals us of the effects of sin. The ultimate victory of sin and death is denied. God's rule of grace and life triumphs.

Communion

We rise form our pews and make our way toward the altar of our salvation. We go forward in union with the great cloud of witnesses who have done so since that first Mass at the Lord's table on Holy Thursday.

As we *receive* the Body and Blood of Christ, we participate in the greatest love story ever told. For when we partake in the Eucharist we are part of God's everlasting love for each of us. The Body and Blood we eat and drink is not like any other food or drink. When we are nourished at the earthly table *we* transform the food and drink according to natural digestion. The Body and Blood of Christ is the eternal food which transforms us in all ways. The Sacrament of God's eternal love transforms and elevates to that Heavenly banquet which never ends.

Our response to having received the Body and Blood of Christ is AMEN, I believe. Nothing more need be said.

After receiving the Body and Blood or Christ we spend some time in *holy silence* expressing our gratitude for the tremendous love shown to us.

Prayer After Communion

We rise to pray that the great mysteries in which we have participated may take deep and lasting root in our lives. Having been nourished by the holy word of Scripture and the Body and Blood of Christ we may be strengthened to live each day as a pleasing offering of gratitude to God.

Concluding Rite

The Concluding Rite consist of two parts: Blessing and Dismissal.

Blessing

The Holy Sacrifice of the Mass opens with the Sign of the Cross. At the end of Mass, we return to the Cross. We live our daily Christian loves in the shadow and power of the Cross. To worldly eyes the Cross is a sign of shame, rejection, and condemnation. To the eyes of faith, the Cross is the sign of Divine Love and salvation.

Dismissal

The faith community who gathers at the beginning of Mass is now the Beloved Community sent forth. The Church is not a hitching post but a sign post. After being nourished by the Word and the Body and Blood of Christ we go forth back into our everyday world. We are <u>not</u> the same as when we gathered for worship. We are sent forth in the power of God to be light in the darkness, salt to a world which only has taste for things below, and heaven so that our world may rise to the things above. We emerge from the church to announce and live the Gospel, strengthened by the Body and Blood of the Savior, and in the peace of the One who is peace itself.

THE MASS

TEACH US TO PRAY:
A Prayer-Filled Journey
with Mary and Jesus

The Judeo-Christian tradition believes that the God of Abraham, Isaac, Jacob, and the Father of Jesus is not indifferent or an absent Creator, but the God of the Bible and the Creed is intimately involved with human history and the human heart. This Divine involvement is not one of manipulation and control as with the Greek gods, rather, the God of the Bible is active through loving care (Divine Providence) and a love which lures us onward. God does not intrude at the expense of our freedom. God invites us into communion with the Divine Life—the Trinity.

Both Jews and Christians profess a strict monotheism when it comes to a belief in God. God is One and He alone is to be worshiped. Granted the Christian tradition proclaims a three-person God. However, the very being of God is One while there are three distinct Persons—Father, Son, and Holy Spirit. Leaving aside these doctrinal differences within the Judeo-Christian tradition, let us focus on the common ground. Namely, the God of Jews and Christians is *personal*. It is personalism which is an essential aspect of the Judeo-Christian tradition, that is, the dignity of the human person is derived from being made in the image and likeness of God (imago Dei).

One may ask what does the Personhood of God and respect for the human person have to do with prayer? This is no insignificant question. For the Bible our Christian faith teaches that the God we worship is involved without being intrusive in history and the lives of the individual. The loving care, involvement by God, is one of invitation to the Divine Persons in the One God. This declaration is crucial since it holds that prayer is an essential component to a fruitful relationship with God. In prayer, we offer our mind and soul, our whole being, to God with a voice of glory, a shout of praise, a heart of gratitude to the Giver of all good gifts, and a cry of petition to the God who is close to the brokenhearted.

For the prayer life and the life of prayer, we turn to our two primary disclosure models—Mary and Jesus. After Mary receives the message from the Archangel Gabriel, we are told she ponders all that happened in heart. Mary was not ponderous (over thinking) but treasured the word of God in her heart. In other words, Mary turned to prayer for wisdom. At the end of the Annunciation episode, she proclaims the words of the perfect disciple: Mary is the true disciple and servant of the Lord.

Mary's Son, the Word Made Flesh, are highly connected in the spiritual cords of prayer. In the Garden of Gethsemane, Jesus experiences a great agony. The disciples are asleep and about to abandon Him (Judas has gone into the night to hand Jesus over and Peter will deny the Lord). The suffering of Jesus is so intense that his sweat contains drops of blood. The Father sends an angel to strengthen Jesus for the final conflict for the day ahead (Good Friday). Jesus requested that the fast approaching cup of suffering may pass. However, Jesus exclaims that He will be faithful to the will of the Father and the mission for which He was sent— redemption through suffering, faithful love.

Both Mary and Jesus are united in a common movement of spirit, namely, a surrender to the will of the Father. This surrender is not one of defeat and withdrawal, rather, their surrender is one of total trust and loving obedience (a true listening heart). Mary and Jesus exhibit the trusting innocence of a child with the maturity possessed by the nature who obey. It is in prayerful trusting obedience that one grows in true freedom. Authentic freedom, rightly understood, is not doing as one wants, but the grace to do and be as one ought. Mary and Jesus show that God's involvement is not the restriction of freedom but, in doing His will, one walks the long road of human liberation. Prayer becomes our own 'yes' to this challenging invitation whereby Christ sets us free.

Two prayers have long been associated with the Catholic-Christian tradition and practice: *the Hail Mary* and the *Our Father*. In the following two sections, we hope to prayerfully revisit both prayers in their own times and what they mean for us today.

The plan is simple and direct: we want to meditate on two of the most familiar, recited, and loved prayers in the Christian tradition—*the Hail Mary* and the *Our Father*. *The Hail Mary* continues to be a bedrock of Catholic piety (the Rosary along with the various Marian devotions) and the *Our Father* enjoys a celebrated place within the offering of each Mass. The Christian Church is a praying Church which draws strength, inspiration, and direction from being in communion with the crucified and risen Lord. The indwelling Holy Spirit sanctifies and sustains the praying, pilgrim Church through history until He comes again.

What follows are two major sections on the life of prayer: Mary and the Hail Mary, and secondly, the response of Jesus through the *Our Father*. Prayer is not one dimensional but comes to the Church through various traditions or streams of flow to the praise of the Father. For example, the Benedictine way is highly liturgical and community centered, the Dominicans focus on the intellectual aspects of prayer, and the Franciscans value the simple (not simplistic). In all of this diversity there is a common thread— praise of the Triune God.

The union, communion if you will, between Mary and Jesus is much deeper than a maternal or biological tie. The deeper current of their bond is spiritual, especially through prayer. The early episodes of Mary's prayer life after the Annunciation is captured by Saint Luke (the Magnificat is a prime example). Overall Mary's approach to prayer is reflective, that is, her ongoing relationship with God is one of reflection and meditation. Likewise, with Jesus, at key moments in His public ministry, He withdraws from the disciples and the external world in order to be alone with the Father. The active ministry draws strength from prayers.

We now commence to begin our prayerful journey with Mary and Jesus; *the Hail Mary* and *Our Father*. The Hope and Purpose Ministries prays that the following pages will be a blessing to you in your Holy Spirit journey.

William F. Maestri

The Hail Mary

The Hail Mary

Hail Mary
Full of grace, the Lord is with thee
Blessed art thou among women and
blessed is the fruit of thy womb, Jesus.
Pray for us sinners, now and at the hour of our death
Amen.

God through His Divine Wisdom and plan selects the most unusual, unexpected, to be vessels of His intentions. God chooses those without formal education and the indwelling Holy Spirit grants the supernatural wisdom. God calls forth the weak and timid and makes them strong. God visits the lowly, by earthly standards, and raises them to those heavenly thrones which do not perish. Why does God do such things? Since we do not know the mind of God we can only speculate. However, if we look to the life and writings of Saint Paul a glimpse emerges, namely, God chooses the 'overlooked' so that there is no cause for *boasting*. The great grace of God's love is not the result of our merit or achievement, rather God's grace is poured forth as a display of the divine goodness.

One would be hard pressed to name a more unlikely candidate for a prime-time role in salvation history than Mary. There is nothing in Mary's resume, but worldly standards, that would indicate that she would provide God with a human face. Her life is simple: Mary is young, a virgin, from an obscure town, and lacking in any formal education in the ways of God. Yet, the ways of God are not the ways of the world. The Archangel Gabriel announces that Mary's yes of faith ('Let it be'), through the indwelling Holy Spirit, will bring forth the Savior to the world.

Hail Mary, Full of Grace

This first prayer (*the Hail Mary*) begins in a way that may give us pause. The natural question arises: why should we hail Mary? On the surface, there is nothing that would evoke Mary for our attention much less our recognition or attention. However, God does not judge by appearances but proves the depth of one's heart. God looks into the heart of Mary and finds one that is pure. Mary's total focus is on doing the will of God. The enticements of the world are secondary. Mary is free because she is God-centered.

There is a deeper reality at work than Mary's pure heart. In typical Marian fashion, our prayer shifts from Mary to the abundant generosity of the Almighty. We offer Mary our greeting, this lowly handmaid, because she is filled with grace. We can hail Mary because of the great things God has done to her and she does for us. The focus is never on her but always directed to God. Mary's proclamation burst from her inner being. God is not simply holy, but God is (His very Being) is holiness itself. Mary dwells on and within the sacred ground of God. She will become the very vessel in whom God dwells.

To conclude this first of the Hail Mary, a brief word about *grace* would seem in order. Such a word is most beneficial for the Catholic community's spirituality. Specifically, many of us came of age in a time when grace-talk was understood more in the language of substance than the language of *relationship*. To be blunt, grace is not like wanting more mashed potatoes placed on our supper plate, rather, grace is that gift which matures and sustains our living relationship with Jesus. During her whole life, Mary has placed that living relationship with God as primary in her life. Mary, we hail you as full of grace—we acknowledge that you are full of grace.

The Lord is with thee.

From the moment of Mary's Immaculate Conception to the time of her glorious Assumption, the Lord is with Mary. With her Annunciation by the Archangel Gabriel, God will take us residence *within* Mary. She will provide God with a human face and be the vessel through whom the world would be granted its Savior. The long march of salvation history, the promise of the Messiah made by God after the expulsion from Eden and to Abraham, would be realized in a stable and crib in Bethlehem. The divine promise had been kept. Mary is at the center of the divine drama.

The road to Bethlehem leads to the foot of the Cross on Calvary. Revealed to us is that God is not only with us, but in the

Person of Jesus, God is **for us**. Mary is present to receive her Son, our Savior, after this dreadful event.

These words—the Lord is with you—seems obvious and reserved only for Mary. Such is not the case. The Lord is with each person whether they know it or not. Through communion with Mary in the Holy Spirit each of us is an incarnational vessel of the Word made flesh. Through our baptism, each of us is to bring Jesus to that part of the world that we touch each day. From home, to work, to school, and the various groups to which we belong, our baptismal vocation calls and empowers us to proclaim the faithful presence of the Lord. This proclamation—God is with us and for us—lies at the center of evangelization. The world is in need of the presence of the Lord. How is this presence revealed? Unlike Caesar, whose image is on a coin, the Person of Jesus is manifest on the Cross at Calvary. Caesar is the love of power. Jesus is the power of love.

Blessed are thou among women

This brief segment of *the Hail Mary* actually contains two parts, one seemingly obvious and the other obscure. The former seems almost self-evident. Of course, Mary is blessed. She is the mother of our Savior. She could not help but be anything but blessed. Jesus was born in a stable in a crib, but before His arrival the one (Mary) who carried Him to birth must be a woman who is sin free (Immaculate Conception) and totally God centered, hence,

40

pure. Mary certainly qualifies. However, we must dig deeper for Mary's blessedness. What is this deeper? Mary's blessedness is pure gift from the gracious hand of the Lord. She never claims to have earned her vocation in salvation history. Rather, understands herself as the lowly handmaid in God has done great things.

The latter part of the Hail Mary—among women—seems puzzling. Mary is blessed among women. What about the rest of women? The Scriptures do **not** indicate they are sinful and unclean. Why is Mary blessed among women? A speculative answer is that this is the opening of Mary's ongoing ministry as the channel through whom God's grace will flow. Mary is not the vessel of grace and blessing for the women of Mary's time, but she will be the ever present faithful for all the generations who will proclaim her as blessed. Mary is the vessel of God's grace for the Church and the individual disciple down through the ages. We see that Mary's blessedness among women, a hint of her ongoing role in redemption.

Mary's blessedness, through unique and supremely intense, extends to the follower of Jesus in every time and place. The blessings we receive from above are not the result of our merit but the Divine goodness. Our blessings are not possession, but as gifts from above which we are meant to share. In our generosity, we participate in God's continuation of doing great things. Holy is God's name.

Blessed is the fruit of thy womb, Jesus

The Hail Mary always points to Jesus, the Word Made Flesh. The Word is conceived, through the Holy Spirit, nurtured, and cared for by the Blessed Mother. In the previous section Mary was declared blessed among women. This was a blessedness that was <u>external</u>, that is, it was a grace that became visible among those who came in contact with Mary. She was the woman for others, especially those in need, the rejected, and the downcast.

The focus of grace and blessedness now shift to the <u>internal</u>. What has made the visible manifestation of grace possible now has taken hold *within* the very body of Mary. Mary's body has become a tabernacle through which the Savior will be delivered to an expectant world. The Word Made Flesh has become enfleshed in the very body of Mary. The God who made promises is the God who is faithful. The fruit of Mary's womb will bring forth the One who will cast mighty from thrones and lift up the lowly. The reversal of earthly ways and values has begun. How can such a thing take place? The womb of Mary, through the overshadowing of the Holy Spirit, carries the One who is light to a world darkened by, and life to a world which has become too comfortable with violence and death. With the Heavenly Host as background, the Savior emerges as the Good News of peace to a hurting world.

The question arises: what does the fruitful womb of Mary mean for us today? From the beginning of creation God fashioned us as material, bodily beings. Our bodily being reaches its zenith with the Incarnation (the Word becomes fully human) and the Resurrection of Jesus (the body is raised up and Holy Spirit filled). Our body is not the tomb of the soul (Plato) but an essential component of our being (a temple in which the Holy Spirit indwells). The womb of Mary reminds us of the pathway to life, even the very life of the Savior. One of the many gifts of women is that they are blessed to serve as the nurturing temple of life from the very first (conception) and throughout the maturation process. Such reverence for the unique gift of women is most relevant during our historical period when the culture of death is in conflict with the civilization of life and love. Mary honors all humankind by welcoming the One who is the Way, the Truth, and the Life. Hail, Mother of Life.

Holy Mary, Mother of God

This brief section of *the Hail Mary* introduces a central theme in the Bible, namely, holiness. God is not just holy, God *is* holiness itself. From the Throne of God flows that grace which sanctifies all of creation. Mary is declared holy because of her calling, that is, she is the mother of God. Mary is pronounced holy, not because of her merit however virtuous she is, rather, Mary is holy because her very body with nurture and bring the Savior—holiness in the flesh.

As always, the focus is on God. Mary participates in the very ground of holiness through the child she is bearing. Mary's child is not ordinary delivery. She is the Mother of God! Jesus is unique in that he is the Son of God and the Savior of the world. No other religious figure or philosopher can claim to be savior. It is *only* Jesus who went to Calvary and rose from the dead. It is only the Risen Lord, Holy Spirit filled, who can raise us to new life. Mary as the Mother of God (Jesus) is embedded in the holiness of God because of her vocation in salvation history—the very human instrument through whom we are saved.

Pope John Paul II taught that our primary path is to walk the ways of everyday holiness. What might this mean? Granted the everyday and routine sounds boring. However, this the long and winding road to communion with the Person of Jesus Christ. The everyday is the holy ground, like Sinai, Bethlehem, Calvary, and the empty tomb at Easter, on which most of us live and move. It is in the daily grind of transforming a house into a home, nurturing children, meeting our work responsibilities, and the various associations to which we belong that we grow in holiness—and yes, sainthood. One of the most powerful insights into holiness (sainthood) was offered by Saint Francis Xavier: the saints were not saints because they do extraordinary things, but because they did the ordinary things extraordinarily well, that is, for the glory and praise of God; for the good of those to whom we can bring that goodness—God. This was said of Mary. May it be said of us.

Pray for us sinners, now and at the hour of our death

We now arrive at the end of *the Hail Mary* by confronting two of the more existential issues, namely, sin and death. Sin is a word that is not in vogue in contemporary culture. Sin has become a linguistic museum piece, that is, something from the long ago covered with dust and cobwebs. Furthermore, the notion of sin has been taken over by the therapeutic culture, and/or, the legal system. Sin is often looked upon as a psychological disorder which requires treatment. Sin, in many quarters, is viewed as a legal and judicial issue which requires punishment or penalty in some form. Against the culture, we must maintain sin as a theological and spiritual reality.

The word sin means to miss the mark or thought. In the theological sense, we deviate from God to travel in search of false gods and the sideways of life. Sin is a fundamental break in our relationship with God. Granted, there is a horizontal dimension to sin, but when our relationship with God is disordered so are our relationships below. The question arises: are we to despair and give in to hopelessness? By no means. We turn to Mary, our Advocate, and Jesus, the Savior.

Looking to Mary may strike one as futile. Why? Mary, by God's special grace, was spared the touch of Original Sin. In going forward, Mary did not experience a bodily death and was assumed into Heaven, body and soul. Hence, we may ask how can Mary relate to us and our human condition? First, Mary was completely human, and the sword of suffering pierced her heart. More importantly, Mary does not stand over and against us in a posture of condemnation, rather, Mary is in solidarity with us in our need. She is not our judge but our advocate before God's throne of Grace. Mary's unique role in salvation history is not distancing from us but a drawing us closer to our true home. Mary has been gifted to us as mother, and her primary show of maternal love is through prayer. In facing the reality of sin, the response must be prayer. Hence, we beseech Mary to pray for us in our sinfulness so that we may open our hearts to the grace of conversion.

The major effect of sin, being apart from God through our free decisions, is death. It is to this topic, within the Hail Mary, that we now turn our attention. The shadow of death haunts our lives from our first to lash breath. The moment of our death can be a time of great fear. *The Hail Mary* turns to Mary in ordered to be strengthened through her prayerful intercession at this time of departure. However, it points us to Jesus, the One who died our death, rose from the dead, and now lives at the right hand of the Father. Into the midst of our death, Mary and Jesus come with the words, "Be not afraid." In other words, at this most vulnerable time it is faith and not fear which is required. How can the fear be driven out? Not by our own will or powers. We are called to turn to a power not of our own making. Mary pints us in the direction of our Savior and her Son. Our gaze is focused on a crib at Bethlehem, a cross on Calvary, and an empty tomb. In so doing, our fear is overcome with the grace of hope. As with the reality of sin, we turn to prayer through the Blessed Mother for the courage to pass from death to life. The Christian community is of the conviction that with death, life is changed and not ended. Mary is with us and for us as she pleads our cause before the throne of God is whom justice and mercy kiss. Fear not!

Amen.

We have come to the end of the body of the Hail Mary. The tradition of our prayers and the reception of the Eucharist calls forth a response from us—Amen. There are variations on this response—"I believe" to "Let it be." The Amen is not just an add on but an expression of faithful surrender to the divine mystery we invoke or receive. The Amen reflects powerfully to the life of Mary. From the Annunciation to the Assumption, and all points before and beyond, Mary's life has been one Amen—I believe and let it as you say. Such is Mary's loving obedience to the will of God.

A question arises, one which Catholics frequently face, namely, do you and the Catholic Church worship Mary? The answer is a resounding *NO*! While the Church and individual Catholic honor Mary, in liturgy and popular piety (for example the Rosary), it is only the Three Person God whom we worship. While some Catholics may speak of Mary in semi-divine terms, Mary would be the first to reject such a display. Here whole life was directed to the Almighty who did great things for her and through her.

A second related question arises, namely, do you Catholics pray to Mary or any of the saints? Again, the answer is a definite No. This response may surprise, if not shock, many Catholics. However, we pray <u>through</u> Mary and the saints to the throne of grace occupied by our Triune God. Mary and the saints are our advocates before God, but they do not take the place, or become equal to, the Almighty. Mary and the saints would have it no other way.

Our attention now turns to the *Our Father*. It is with this prayer, liturgically and in everyday piety, that we turn to the Father of us all.

The Our Father

The Lord's Prayer
(The Our Father)

Our Father, Who art in Heaven,
Hallowed be Thy Name.
Thy Kingdom come.
Thy Will be done, on earth as it is in Heaven.
Give us this day our daily bread.
And forgive us our trespasses,
as we forgive those who trespass against us.
And lead us not into temptation,
but deliver us from evil.
For the Kingdom, the power and the glory are yours,
now and forever.
Amen.

The *Our Father* emerges from a rather surprising request from Jesus' disciples—teach us to pray. This is unexpected since prayer has been a fundamental component in the Jewish historical experience. Hence, we must ask why would the disciples ask Jesus to school them in prayer? After all, Jesus was not a trained rabbi, nor was Jesus a synagogue official. He was a traveling preacher and teacher with no official religious standing; except the authority that flowed from His Presence.

The disciples have on occasion witnessed the communion between Jesus and the Father. They experienced the renewed Jesus after spending time alone in prayer. The disciples knew that there was a deeper level of oneness with God. They knew that Jesus had connected with a deeper force. The disciples desired to be in touch with this special grace. They believed that way to such a gift was found in the Person of Jesus.

It is not unexpected that Jesus teaches the prayer that directs our minds and hearts to the Father. Jesus' mission and ministry were grounded in doing the will of the Father. The prayer taught by Jesus to the disciples, and those who will follow down through the ages, is offered to the Father, Jesus' Father is <u>ours</u> as well.

The body of the *Our Father* is comprised of a series of petitions. As we shall see in the following sections, all of our supplications are directed to the Father. The *Our Father* is not only a prayer for the individual believer but is a key part in the celebration of the Eucharist. The Lord's Prayer is not something we mindlessly say or race through, rather, it is prayerful preparation of the soul to receive the Real Presence of Jesus in the Eucharist.

It is to the *Our Father* that we now turn.

Our Father

From the opening of the Lord's Prayer, we need to pay attention to specific words, namely, the use of the collective pronounced 'our'. This reminds us that God is the Father of us all and we are bound together beyond race, ethnicity, religion, and all of the divisions that have come to separate us, one from another. With God as our Father we are united spiritually in one family. The grace received by one member strengthens the Church as a whole. Likewise, the sin of one weakens the Church's mission. Through the cycles of grace and sin, there is one constant, namely, we remain the people of God.

With the acknowledgement of God as our Father, we are in communion with Jesus who came to do the Father's will. The opening of the Lord's Prayer is a reminder of who we and whose we are. Our life is not our own. We belong to another and Our Heavenly Father. This relationship with the Father does not mean that our freedom and identity are eliminated. Quite the contrary. In our prayerful oneness with the Father we receive the true freedom that only God can grant. We become increasingly liberated from the slavery to self and the ever-changing currents of the culture. It is in our Father that we find a safe harbor and stability which promotes freedom. Furthermore, in the presence of the Father we are given the grace to become who God intended us to be. As Jesus taught, when we die to ourselves we become the person fully alive to the glory of the Father.

Who art in Heaven

These few words invite us to a deep mystery, namely, that the Father is above, that is, God is not reducible to one object among others of the created, finite order. In Him and through Him all of existence has its being. The Father is the Creator of Heaven and earth. However, when we reference the transcendence of the Father we are not talking about the distance or indifference of God to the creation or human family. Rather, the Father's 'otherness' is one of providential care for all that He has spoken into existence and sustains by the Divine love. The transcendence of the Almighty, the Ancient One, is at the same time One of involvement with <u>all</u> of creation.

Within the Old and New testament there is a great deal of talks about <u>fear</u>. In fact, one of the gifts of the Holy Spirit is 'fear of the Lord.' Why should we fear the Lord? The fear of which the Bible speaks is not one which calls us to flee, rather, it is an invitation to adoration. We are summoned to acknowledge the supreme greatness of God in comparison to ourselves and the created order. Biblical fear is more akin to awe and adoration towards the God who lives in unapproachable light. The Father to whom we pray, and who resides in Heaven, cannot be bound by the confines of finite earthly space and time. The infinity of Heaven reflects the ultimacy that is the Father. Jesus teaches that we direct our prayers to the Father in whom all blessings flow. In the fulness of time the Throne of Grace will become visible in the greatest of gifts, namely, the Word made flesh, our Savior Jesus the Christ.

Hallowed be Thy Name

As we travel the pages of the Bible, we come up a constant—God is HOLY. More specifically, God is the very ground of holiness itself. When Moses encounters God on Sinai, Moses is told he is standing on holy ground. At the celebration of the Eucharist we proclaim that God is holy. This is not an idle filler of word, but a declaration of the very reality of God. God is holiness, otherness, from all that is created.

The concept of name is crucial in our general biblical framework. The notion of name is much more than an individual designation. To name someone or something is to reveal the very nature or essence of that which is named. The one who has the authority (a moral reality) to name exercises a great power and responsibility. It falls to Adam to name the various animals in Eden. When Moses encounters God on Mount Sinai he asks God (the burning bush) for His name (what shall we call you?). God of course declines. God will not surrender His name for that would transfer power from God to humans. It is God in His supreme goodness orders all thing natural purpose for His glory.

The Holy Name of God is not locked in Heaven. To walk in the name of God, as His family, is to walk in the way of holiness. To travel the way of holiness, saintly living, is not a withdrawal from daily life. On the contrary, it is to immerse oneself deeply in the marrow of everyday existence. The ordinary and grinding routine is the everyday marrow in which God is to be found. Saint Francis Xavier teaches that the Saints were not Saints because they did extraordinary things, but they did the ordinary things extraordinarily well. The way into God's Holy Name is found in the everyday joys and burdens we face. When we accept the everyday realities with love for God and service to others, we draw even closer to God and to our vocation to be holy as God is holy.

Thy Kingdom come

The Kingdom of God (heaven in Matthew) is the central preaching of Jesus of Nazareth. This Kingdom is not geographical or political, it is not confined by space and time. Rather, God's Kingdom is the <u>active</u> rule of God in the lives and hearts of individuals. Granted, the reign of God has consequences in the public realm. Jesus, the embodiment of the Kingdom, cure of the sick and expelled evil spirits as a sign that the Kingdom was among them in the Person of Jesus.

The proclamation of the Kingdom of God by Jesus needs to be appreciated in detail. In the Gospel of Mark (Mark 1:14-15) we read: "This is the time of fulfillment. The Kingdom of God is at hand. Repent, and believe in the gospel." It would be fruitful, within the context of the *Our Father*, to explore Jesus' preaching as it relates to the Kingdom of God.

a) <u>The time of fulfillment</u>

The Jewish people are the ones of God's promise—the Covenant. The Father is forever faithful to His Word. However, the Covenant is realized in an unexpected way and with an abundance of grace—the Word Became Flesh. Jesus is the living presence of the Kingdom of God. Hence, He acts and teaches with authority, that is, Jesus' public ministry is carried out with a moral and spiritual aspect that is lacking in the customary leaders of the day.

The time of fulfillment is not only one of promise keeping by the Father, but this Covenant promise is kept in the Person of Jesus. The Kingdom of God is the very active presence of the Father, in the Person of Jesus, and though the indwelling of the Holy Spirit. In other words, the time of fulfillment is Trinitarian. The preaching of the Kingdom and the Person of Jesus as the reign of the Father is not frozen in time. This preaching blows down to us.

Through our baptism in the Holy Spirit we are born anew. Our human birth gives way to our supernatural rebirth in the Lord. Through an aging grace we become a new creation. There are two kingdoms before us (Saint Augustine) the earthly kingdom and the Kingdom of God. The foundation of the worldly kingdom is founded on force and power. The Kingdom of God, in the Person of Jesus, is grounded in the power of love, forgiveness, and peace. Which path will we walk? This decision brings us to our next part.

b) the Kingdom of God is at hand.

In the Person of Jesus, the Kingdom of God becomes visible and present. It is a time for one to make a decision. There is no more "later" or convenient hour. There is a sense of urgency. A commitment is always difficult because it seems like a loss of freedom. Such is not the case. The opposite is true, for only the mature can commit to something or someone. Genuine liberty comes to those who have the will to say 'yes'. It is in the Kingdom of God that we walk in the liberty that Christ has set us free.

c) Repent and believe in the gospel

The *Our Father* invites us to an uncomfortable place. Namely, we are being called to change. At a deeper level we are being summoned to metanoia, that is, an openness to the ways of God that transforms the very core of our being, we cannot so this conversion by our own power. We must rely on the gracious grace of the Father to experience a change of heart.

Repentance is the pathway to faith in the gospel of Jesus. We need to be clean about the meaning of faith. Namely, faith is a supernatural gift from God which enlightens the mind and strengthens the will. The grace of faith is much more than learning the doctrines and dogmas of the Church. Faith is a way of life in which we daily leave our nets and walk in the footsteps of the Teacher, to the praise of the Father, in the indwelling power of the Holy Spirit.

Repentance (conversion), which leads to a living faith, prepares us to accept and live the good news of gospel salvation. The good news is found in the Person of Jesus who assures us that he is the Way, the Truth, and the Life. Faith is not only a movement of the mind. A living faith, God's gift, is the movement of one's whole being to the Person of Jesus. The grace of conversion is grounded in humanism, that is, each person encounters the Person of Jesus the Word made flesh.

Thy will be done on earth as it is in Heaven.

We now encounter a challenging patch of the Lord's prayer. Specifically, we pray for the Father's will to be done. Why is this so difficult? From the time of Original Sin, we humans have assented our will over and in conflict with the Divine Will. This struggle of wills continues throughout human history and within ourselves. We petition to that grace which strengthens us to surrender to the will of the Father in loving obedience. It is not a surrender of defeat, rather, it is a dying to self-promotion which liberates us to be with and for God and others.

To do the will of the Father we turn our gaze to Mary and the Person of Jesus. Although Mary is deeply troubled by the Archangel Gabriel's announcement, she gives voice to all who would be a disciple—let it be. Mary who also expresses the mission of the whole Church, namely, to serve as the sign of Jesus' presence in the world. When we turn to the Savior we see the same dynamic. Namely, Jesus, in perfect obedience, surrenders to the will of his Father. Jesus will accept the baptism of fire and drink from the chalice of suffering with is near at hand.

Each day, in so many ways, the Father invites us to a loving communion with His holy will. There are times when the Lord's word will trouble us, and like many we will be called to ponder the word and treasure it in our hearts. All of us are called, at one point, to drink from the cup of challenge in our daily life. In both instances we are invited to surrender to the will of the Father. Again, this is not a loss of freedom but a journey in liberty whereby Christ has made us free.

Give us this day our daily bread

The God we call "Our Father" is the One who pours gifts into the hem of our garments. We implore the Given of gifts for what we need (not want) today. Too often we live in fast forward and over-look the blessings and needs that are before us. The Lord's Prayer turns our attention to the importance of the need for 'daily bread'. What is this everyday nourishment we need? In today's culture, we are over fed and under nourished. Most of us would not participate in an athletic event, or engage in personal fitness, without proper preparation (food, water, and warm ups). The same is true for our spiritual life. We need the support, daily, of the Sacred Scriptures. The Bible strengthens us for the everyday demands of life.

Secondly, we need to be engaged, daily, in the reading of spiritual or religious literature, from the Church fathers to competent present-day writers. Thirdly, we need the daily discipline of prayer and meditation. We need to focus on the things above. Through the Holy Spirit, we focus our total being on the Father who is the Supreme Being. Finally, we must, as often as possible, be nourished at the Lord's table (altar) in the Eucharist. It is the *real* presence, Body, Blood, and divinity, which we are offered for the journey of discipleship on earth and into eternal life.

Forgive us our trespasses

Sin is a part of our inheritance since the Fall in Eden. Yes, Jesus took all of our sin and guilt to Calvary. Yet, we know the battle continues. It is only God who can forgive sin. Why? Because sin is vertical, that is, an offence against the abundant goodness and grace of our merciful God. We place our will above the will of the Father. This is an old story going all the way to that first garden of the earthly paradise. Yes, there was the banishment but also a promise of redemption. And this promise is kept through Mary and the power of the Holy Spirit. Jesus, the Word made flesh, offers the forgiveness of the Father. Jesus is the totally innocent Lamb who offers himself as the perfect sacrifice. The sacrifice of Jesus on the Cross to the Father is unblemished. Jesus on Calvary reveals the compassion of the Father as suffering, enduring love. For it is only in generosity of the Father that we are healed.

When we offend our Heavenly Father, such transgressions effect our everyday relationships—home, work, and the many associations to which we are involved. When we offend our Heavenly Father, we experience a brokenness within our most intimate and casual relationships. As our Heavenly Father forgives us, we are to forgive others. It is to this second part of the 'forgiveness clause' that we now turn.

As we forgive those who trespass against us

There is a profound connection between the Father's forgiveness of us and our extending pardon to one another. Forgiveness is not something (a grace) we hold on to as a private possession, rather, the divine forgiveness overflows to others. Because of our sinful nature, we have received, and in need, of the infinite mercy of the Father. As we have received so we are to extend to others.

However, this flow of forgiveness from God to us, and we to others requires difficult steps, namely, the grace to <u>forget</u> as we forgive. The part can be a heavy collar which presents us from walking in the steps of Jesus. A forgiving memory (healing of memories) is granted by openness to the Holy Spirit, whose indwelling presence empowers us to move past the past. Regret and resentment do not move us to that future to hope in to which the Lord's grace invites us. Yes, there may be experiences in our life which have left scars; however, our scars can become stars. We can, through grace, be a shining light to others who experience only darkness. We can be a witness to the Savior who is that Light and Life who shines in the darkness of despair and is not overcome.

Lead us not into temptation, but deliver us from evil.

One must admit that the request not to encounter temptation is rather strange. Why would the Father bring us to the point of temptation? It must be remembered that before Jesus' public ministry, He was led by the Holy Spirit into the desert to confront Satan (the Accuser and Deceiver). Throughout His ministry, Jesus contends with Satan until His final victory on the Cross and with the empty tomb (Resurrection). It is important to remember that *strength comes through the struggle*. Even Jesus faced many challenges—doubt, rejection, condemnation, and the attempts to kill Him; which needed to be overcome to do the will of the Father.

At the same time, we face many temptations for which by ourselves, we do not possess the resources to resist. What this part of the Lord's Prayer is requesting is that we will not succumb to these daily temptings to stray from the path of the Lord. The everyday grind and routines of life can be a burden. Without prayer for the strength of grace, we can easily follow the wrong road. We beseech the Father for His blessings of strength to continue the journey.

The two prayers we have been reflecting on, the *Hail Mary* and the *Our Father*, converge at the time of our most vulnerable, namely, the hour of our death. If we are honest we must admit that fear is strong and even the strongest of courageous hope can be shaken by the forces of darkness. Hence, we petition the Blessed Mother to pray for us as death inches closer. In *the Lord's Prayer*, we turn to Jesus for deliverance from the evil one. That is, we beseech the Father to grant those graces which keep us strong in faith, resolute in hope, and confident in the Father's everlasting love. When the time of our death draws near, or if the presence of the evil one becomes more pronounced, may we look to Calvary. With blessed assurance, may we receive that grace which tells us, "Be not afraid. I have overcome the sting of death. In communion with Me you will have life, and have life in abundance."

For the kingdom, the power and the glory are yours, now and forever. Amen.

This sentence is added in at the end of the *Our Father* during Mass. The Kingdom attests to God's active rule in all of history and all human hearts. The Kingdom that Jesus preached is an everlasting Kingdom, not a temporal or temporary reign. It is an eternal Kingdom. The eternal rule of God, in hearts and history, in God's creation. The power is the power of God's presence through the indwelling presence of the Holy Spirit. The Glory is the acknowledgement of God's almighty gifts. And of God's supreme being in all of Creation. It is for ever and ever, Amen.

A Concluding Note

In the proceeding pages, we reflected on two of the most popular prayers through the Christian centuries. However, there is a thread which connects Mary and Jesus. Namely, *the Hail Mary* and *the Lord's Prayer* were more than words, the Blessed Mother and the Word made flesh are profound expressions of lives totally devoted to loving obedience to the Father's will. There comes at a crucial time when prayer, however profound, passes from word to action. Without a bodily expression of our prayers they remain just words which render our spirituality lifeless. The Word became embodied in Mary. The Father did not effect saving love at a distance, but Jesus entered our history and hearts fully human. Love, like prayer, seeks contact with the beloved in order to show a bodily expression of commitment. The Father is not only with us but for us. The Blessed Mother and Jesus are also with us and for us. Our voices cry, AMEN!

Dear Reader,

We hope that this book has been a blessing in your life. To learn more about Hope and Purpose Ministries and how you can become involved, please visit our website at: www.HopeAndPurpose.org.

Thank you and may God continue to bless you abundantly.

The Hope and Purpose Ministries Team

OTHER RESOURCES FROM
HOPE AND PURPOSE MINISTRIES

Books:
A Heart Renewed (Lent)
A Time to Wait; A Time for Hope (Advent)
Preaching Jesus by Deacon Larry Oney and Fr. William Maestri
Reflections on the Kingdom of God by Deacon Larry Oney
Up Faith! by Deacon Larry Oney

Videos (DVDs):
4th International Priests' Retreat in East Africa
Amos and the Poor
Discerning & Walking in Your Divine Mission
Discovering Your Divine Mission
Entering Your Divine Mission
Extraordinary Mercy
Faith and Marriage
Hosanna
Participation in the Ministry of Jesus
Returning to My Father's House Revival
Stirring up the Gifts
Succeeding in Your Divine Mission
The Baptism of Jesus
Walking in Your Divine Mission
Walking in Your Supernatural Anointing

Audio (CDs):

4th International Priests' Retreat in East Africa
A Teaching for Leaders
Amos and the Poor
Behold the Lamb
Christian Prayer
Divine Assignment
Divine Preparation
Extraordinary Mercy
Faith and Marriage
Faith as a Gift from God
Faith as a Response to God
Faith as an Act Toward God
Hosanna 2014
How to Receive and Pray for Healing-Part One
How to Receive and Pray for Healing-Part Two
Participation in the Ministry of Jesus
Repent and Believe in the Good News
Seeing with Spiritual Eyes
Stirring up the Gifts of the Holy Spirit
Strengthen Your Marriage
The Baptism of Jesus
The Glory of God
The Kingdom of God
The Power of God
The Profession of Faith
The Purpose of a Retreat
Walking in Your Supernatural Anointing

Made in the USA
Columbia, SC
05 August 2018